CONTENTS

Words in **bold** can be found in the glossary on page 28

Changing materials

Everything around you is made up of materials. Everyday materials include wood, plastic, metal and fabrics. Materials change all around you everyday. Ice turns to water in drinks and wood burns on bonfires.

↓ *Snow and ice change to water when they warm up.*

Changing
Materials

Chris Oxlade

WAYLAND

First published in Great Britain in 2006 by Wayland,
an imprint of Hachette Children's Books

Copyright © 2006 Wayland

Hachette Children's Books
338 Euston Road, London NW1 3BH

Editor: Hayley Leach
Senior Design Manager: Rosamund Saunders
Designer: Ben Ruocco
Photographer: Philip Wilkins

British Library Cataloguing in Publication Data
Oxlade, Chris
    Changing materials. - (Working with materials)
    1.Chemistry, Technical - Juvenile literature
    I.Title
    660

ISBN-10: 0-7502-4903-x
ISBN-13: 978-0-7502-4903-4

Cover photograph: a glassblower cuts molten glass.
Photo credits: Jeri Gleiter/Getty Images 6, Janine Wiedel
Photolibrary/Alamy 7, Lynne Siler Photography/Alamy 8,
Japack/Photolibrary.com 9, Howard Sayer/Alamy 10,
Simon Belcher/Alamy 11, John Zoiner/Photolibrary.com 12,
Marc Moritsch/National Geographic/Getty Images 13,
Stephen Toner/Getty Images 14, Tim Thiel/Getty Images 15,
Ronnie Kaufman/Corbis 16, Elizabeth Simpson/Getty Images 17,
Chris Everard/Getty Images 18, Richard Hutching/Science
Photo Library cover and 19, Niall McDiarmid/Alamy 20, Philip
Wilkins 21, Peter Cade/Getty Images 22, Stefan Mokrzecki/
Photolibrary.com 23, Manor Photography/Alamy 24,
Shout/Alamy 25, Philip Wilkins 26-27.

The publishers would like to thank the models Philippa and Sophie
Campbell for appearing in the photographs.

Imagine biscuits baking, a candle burning and ice melting. These materials are changing. The biscuits are turning hard, the candle wax is being used up and the ice is turning to water.

↑ These pots were heated in a **kiln**. The soft clay has turned hard.

Changing shape

A solid material is a material that stays in the same shape. Wood and plastic are solid materials. We can change the shape of solid materials by pulling and pushing on them. We can make these materials squash, stretch, bend or twist.

↓ *Each bow is made of solid plastic. They bend when the archers pull the bow string.*

← *Water is a liquid. It takes the shape of the container it goes into.*

It's a Fact!

Slime from a joke shop is like a solid and a liquid. It flows like a liquid. If you press it hard it stays in shape like a solid.

A liquid is a material that changes shape by itself. If you put some liquid into a container, the liquid flows and fills up the bottom of the container.

Bending and breaking

When you stretch, squash, bend or twist materials, such as modelling clay or bread dough, they stay in their new shape. Some materials return to their original shape. For example, an elastic band springs back into shape when you stop pulling it.

← It is easy to make new shapes with modelling clay.

*↑ Chocolate hardly bends at all before it snaps. We say that it is a **brittle** material.*

It's a Fact!

A spring is a coil of strong wire. It springs back into shape after it is squashed or stretched. Cars and pens have springs inside.

Some materials are easier to squash, stretch, bend and twist than others. Rubber is easy to bend, wood is harder to bend and metal is very difficult to bend. Materials can break if we try to change their shape too much.

Melting materials

Ice is a solid material and water is a liquid. When a material changes from a solid to a liquid, we say that it melts. Melting happens when a solid material gets warmer. Ice cubes melt because they warm up outside the freezer.

← Metals are melted so they can be made into new shapes in **moulds**.

← When **molten lava** from a volcano cools it turns to solid rock.

The reverse of melting is called freezing or solidifying. This is when a liquid turns to a solid. Freezing happens when a liquid material is cooled down. When you put water in a freezer, the water cools down. This makes it freeze and turn to ice.

Boiling materials

When water is heated in a pan the water gets hotter and hotter. In the end, bubbles of gas come up from the bottom of the pan. Some of the water is changing into gas. This change is called boiling. The gas is called water vapour or steam.

↓ A boiling mud pool. Deep underground, water is turning to steam that bubbles up through the mud.

← Water vapour is hitting this pan lid as the water boils. The water vapour cools quickly and turns back to water.

A gas can turn to liquid, too. This change is called **condensation**. Boiling water in a pan turns to water vapour. Above the pan the vapour cools down. It turns back to tiny water droplets.

15

Water vapour in the air

After it rains the ground is wet and puddles form. If the sun's heat dries the ground the puddles disappear. This is because water turns into water vapour and mixes with the air. This change is called **evaporation**.

↓ *These paints are runny because they contain water. The paint dries when the water evaporates.*

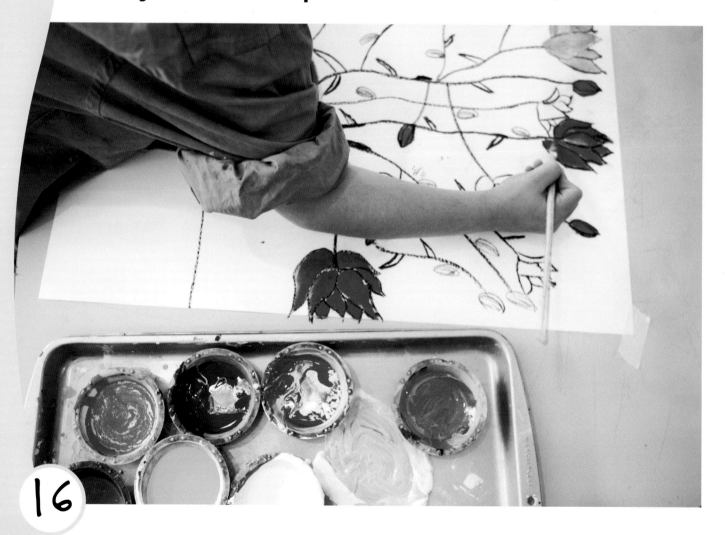

16

↑ *Clouds are made of tiny drops of water. The drops are made when water vapour in the air cools down.*

There is always some water vapour in the air. When the air cools down some of the water vapour turns back to liquid water which forms clouds. On a hot day, the air around a can of cold drink cools down and small drops of water appear on the can.

Hard and soft

When ice melts, it turns straight from solid ice to liquid water. When some materials are heated up they just get softer and softer before turning into a liquid. Chocolate and butter go soft in a warm room.

↓ *This butter has become soft enough to spread.*

↑ *Glass goes soft when it is very hot.*

Materials that go soft when they are heated are easy to make into shapes. A chocolate bar is made by pouring hot, **runny** chocolate into a mould. When the chocolate cools down it goes hard, making a solid bar.

It's a Fact!

Plastic objects, such as plastic drinks bottles, are made in moulds. Hot, runny plastic is put into a mould. Then the mould is cooled making the plastic go hard.

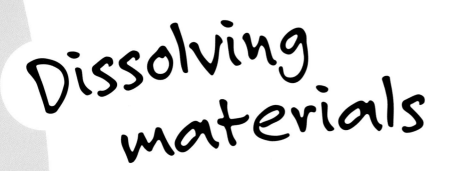

Dissolving materials

Salt is often added to water for cooking vegetables. The grains of salt gradually break up into pieces that are too small to see. When a material breaks up in water like this we say that it **dissolves**. The mixture of the salt and water is called a **solution**.

← *When you stir sugar into a drink, the sugar dissolves in the liquid.*

← These crystals of salt formed when a solution of water and salt dried up.

It's a Fact!

We can't clean oily paints from brushes with water. Instead we use a liquid called white spirit. Oil dissolves in white spirit but not in water.

We can get the dissolved material out of a solution by taking away the water. If we leave a dish of solution in a warm place the water gradually evaporates (see page 16). When all the water has gone the material is left in the dish.

Changing forever

Changes such as squashing and melting can be **reversed**. An elastic band can return to shape and water can be frozen to make ice again. Some changes cannot be reversed. For example, when an egg is cooked it changes forever.

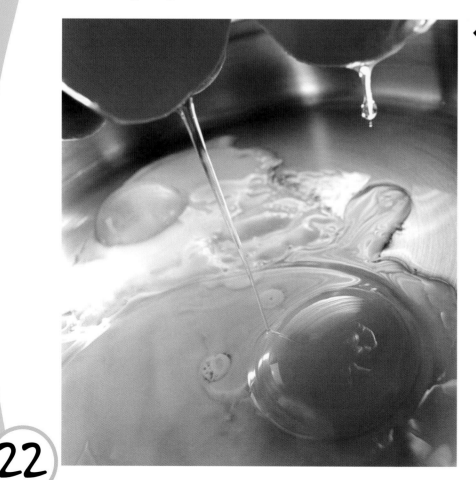

← Heating an egg makes the egg go solid. This change can never be reversed.

← *Material changes happen naturally, too. These leaves gradually change as they rot away.*

It's a Fact!

When cement, water, sand and gravel are mixed together they change into a new material called concrete.

When you bake a cake a permanent change happens. The ingredients in the cake mixture, such as sugar and flour, are changed into new materials that make up the baked cake.

Burning materials

When a candle burns, the wax in the candle changes forever. As it changes it makes heat and light that come from the flame. Burning is a useful way to change materials. We use it to make heat for cooking and for keeping warm.

↓ Wood burns on a fire. The wood is turned into ash.

↑ *Foam stops oxygen getting to the burning material so the fire goes out.*

Burning can't happen without **oxygen** in the air. Fire-fighters often put out a fire by covering the burning material. They cover it with **foamy** water or a blanket.

It's a Fact!

A fuel is a material that we burn on purpose to make heat. Gas, coal and wood are all fuels.

Activities

Making salt crystals

Try this experiment to see how evaporation works.

What you need	
glass bowl	table salt
plastic saucer	tea spoon

① Put 250 millilitres of warm (not hot) water in the glass bowl.

② Put in a teaspoon of table salt. Stir until the salt dissolves.

③ Keep adding teaspoons of salt one at a time and stir. Stop adding salt when you can't make it dissolve.

④ Pour a little of the salt solution onto a plastic saucer and leave the saucer in a warm place.

⑤ Look at the saucer every hour and write down what you see. How much of the water has gone? Can you see any salt? After a few hours all the water will have gone. It has evaporated. The salt from the solution is left on the saucer.

Making plastic

Find out how you can make plastic using everyday materials.

What you need

non-skimmed milk   coffee filter
vinegar   dessert spoon
plastic dish

① Put four dessert spoons of milk in a plastic bowl.

② Add one dessert spoon of vinegar. Stir the milk and vinegar together.

③ Pour the mixture into a coffee filter. Leave the filter over the bowl for about 15 minutes. Clear liquid will ooze out of the filter.

④ The white solid left in the filter is a type of plastic. It was made when the vinegar and milk changed when they were mixed together.

⑤ Leave the filter in a warm place. When the plastic dries it will feel hard.

Glossary

brittle something which snaps easily

condensation when a gas turns into a liquid

dissolve to break up into tiny pieces in a liquid

evaporate when a liquid changes to a gas

foam a material made up of many bubbles joined to each other

kiln a large oven used for making clay hard

lava hot, molten rock from a volcano

molten when something is heated until it melts

mould a block of material with a space inside. When molten material is poured into a mould it forms an object the shape of the space.

oxygen a gas found in the air

runny when something flows like a liquid

reversed when something is changed back to what it was before

solution a liquid with another material dissolved in it

Further information

BOOKS

How We Use: Metals/Paper/Rubber/Wood
by Chris Oxlade, Raintree (2005)

A Material World: It's Glass/It's Metal/It's Plastic/It's Wood
by Kay Davies and Wendy Oldfield, Wayland (2006)

Investigating Science: How do we use materials?
by Jacqui Bailey, Franklin Watts (2005)

WEBSITES

www.bbc.co.uk/schools/revisewise/science/materials/09_act.shtml
Animated examples and quiz about changing materials

www.strangematterexhibit.com
Fun site about the properties of materials

PLACES TO VISIT

Eureka, Halifax
www.eureka.org.uk

Glasgow Science Centre
www.glasgowsciencecentre.org

The Science Museum, London
www.sciencemuseum.org.uk

Index